Data Structures and Algorithms in Python

Hernando Abella

Aluna Publishing House is united by our shared passion for education, languages, and technology. Our mission is to provide the ultimate learning experience when it comes to books. We believe that books are not just words on paper; they are gateways to knowledge, imagination, and enlightenment.

Through our collective expertise, we aim to bridge the gap between traditional learning and the digital age, harnessing the power of technology to make books more accessible, interactive, and enjoyable. We are dedicated to creating a platform that fosters a love for reading, language, and lifelong learning. Join us on our journey as we embark on a quest to redefine the way you experience books.

Let's unlock the limitless potential of knowledge, one page at a time.

Table of contents

Introduction to Data Structures and Algorithms 5

What is an algorithm? 6

Why learn data structures and algorithms? 7

Fundamentals of Programming with Python 9

    Basic Python programming concepts 10
    Variables and Data Types 12
    Control Flow 14
    Functions and recursion 16
    Exception Handling 18

Basic Data Structures 20

    Lists 21
    Tuples 24
    Dictionaries 26
    Sets 29

Elementary Algorithms 32

    Sorting Algorithms 33
    Searching algorithms 35
    Mathematical Algorithms: 38
    String Algorithms: 40
    Recursion: 41

Introduction to Data Structures 42

    Stack 43
    Queue 46
    Linked List 49

More Data Structures 53

    Hash table 54

Trees...56
Graphs...61
Practical Applications...63
Problem-solving strategies...64
Real-world examples of data structures and
  algorithms...77

Introduction to Data Structures and Algorithms

What is an algorithm?

An algorithm is a step-by-step procedure or set of rules designed to solve a specific problem or perform a particular task. It's essentially a sequence of well-defined instructions that can be executed to achieve a desired outcome.

Algorithms can be found everywhere in our daily lives, from simple tasks like making a sandwich to complex processes like search engines ranking web pages or GPS navigation systems finding the best route. In computer science, algorithms are crucial for solving problems efficiently, organizing and manipulating data, and designing software systems.

Key characteristics of algorithms include:

Input: Algorithms typically take some input data, which they process to produce an output.

Output: The result produced by the algorithm after processing the input.

Definiteness: Each step of the algorithm must be precisely defined and unambiguous.

Finiteness: The algorithm must eventually terminate after a finite number of steps.

Effectiveness: Every step of the algorithm must be feasible and computable using available resources.

Correctness: The algorithm should produce the correct output for all valid inputs.

Optimality: An optimal algorithm produces the best possible result within given constraints (e.g., time, space).
Algorithms can be expressed in various forms, such as natural language descriptions, pseudocode, flowcharts, or actual code in a programming language. They are fundamental to the field of computer

science and play a crucial role in problem-solving, software development, and computational thinking.

Why learn data structures and algorithms?

Learning data structures and algorithms is essential for several reasons:

Problem-solving skills: Data structures and algorithms provide foundational problem-solving techniques that are applicable across various domains of computer science and beyond. They teach you how to break down complex problems into smaller, more manageable tasks and devise efficient solutions.

Efficiency and optimization: Understanding data structures and algorithms enables you to develop more efficient and optimized software solutions. By choosing the right data structures and implementing algorithms with lower time and space complexity, you can improve the performance of your programs, making them faster and more scalable.

Critical thinking and analytical skills: Studying data structures and algorithms requires logical reasoning and analytical thinking. You'll learn how to analyze problems, identify patterns, and devise algorithmic solutions. These skills are valuable not only in programming but also in various fields that require analytical problem-solving abilities.

Foundation for software engineering: Data structures and algorithms serve as the building blocks of software engineering. They provide the underlying infrastructure for designing and implementing complex software systems, including databases, compilers, operating systems, and more.

Interview preparation: Many technical interviews for software engineering positions include questions on data structures and algorithms. By mastering these concepts, you'll be better prepared to tackle interview questions, solve coding challenges, and demonstrate your problem-solving skills to potential employers.

Understanding existing codebases: Knowledge of data structures and algorithms helps you understand and analyze existing codebases more effectively. You'll be able to identify and optimize inefficient algorithms, refactor code for better performance, and contribute meaningfully to software development projects.

Foundational knowledge for further learning: Data structures and algorithms serve as the foundation for learning more advanced topics in computer science, such as artificial intelligence, machine learning, cryptography, and parallel computing. Having a solid understanding of these fundamentals will facilitate your exploration of more specialized areas in the field.

Fundamentals of Programming with Python

Basic Python programming concepts

Variables and Data Types: Variables are used to store data in Python. Python supports various data types, including integers, floats, strings, booleans, lists, tuples, dictionaries, and sets.

```python
# Example of variable declaration and data types
age = 25      # integer
height = 5.9  # float
name = "John"   # string
is_student = True  # boolean
```

Control Flow: Control flow statements allow you to control the execution flow of your Python code. Common control flow statements include if-elif-else statements, loops (for and while loops), and break and continue statements.

```python
# Example of if-elif-else statement
num = 10
if num > 0:
    print("Positive")
elif num == 0:
    print("Zero")
else:
    print("Negative")
```

Functions: Functions are reusable blocks of code that perform a specific task. They help organize code and promote code reuse.

```python
# Example of a function
def greet(name):
    print("Hello, " + name + "!")

greet("Alice")
```

Lists, Tuples, and Dictionaries: These are built-in data structures in Python.

- **Lists:** Ordered collections of items that can be modified (mutable).
- **Tuples:** Similar to lists but immutable (cannot be changed after creation).
- **Dictionaries:** Key-value pairs that allow you to access values by their associated keys.

```
# Examples of lists, tuples, and dictionaries
my_list = [1, 2, 3, 4, 5]
my_tuple = (1, 2, 3)
my_dict = {"name": "John", "age": 30, "city": "New York"}
```

Loops: Loops are used to iterate over a sequence of items. Python supports for loops and while loops.

```
# Example of a for loop
for i in range(5):
    print(i)

# Example of a while loop
num = 5
while num > 0:
    print(num)
    num -= 1
```

Input and Output: Python provides built-in functions for taking user input and displaying output.

```
# Example of input and output
name = input("Enter your name: ")
print("Hello, " + name + "!")
```

Variables and Data Types

Variables: A variable is a symbolic name that represents a value stored in the computer's memory.

Variables are created using the assignment operator (=).

Python is dynamically typed, meaning you don't need to explicitly declare the data type of a variable.

Variable names should be descriptive and follow certain naming conventions (e.g., use lowercase letters, underscores for spaces, avoid starting with numbers).

Data Types:

Python supports several built-in data types, including:

Numeric Types:

- **int:** Integer values (e.g., 10, -5, 1000).
- **float:** Floating-point values (e.g., 3.14, -0.001, 2.0).
- **String:** Represents sequences of characters enclosed within single (') or double (") quotes (e.g., 'Hello', "Python", '123').

Strings are immutable, meaning they cannot be changed once created.
Boolean:

Represents boolean values True and False. These are used for logical operations and comparisons.

List: Ordered collection of items, which can be of different data types.

Created using square brackets ([]) and items separated by commas (e.g., [1, 2, 3], ['apple', 'banana', 'orange']).

Tuple: Similar to lists but immutable (cannot be changed after creation).

Created using parentheses (()) and items separated by commas (e.g., (1, 2, 3), ('apple', 'banana', 'orange')).

Dictionary: Collection of key-value pairs, where each key is associated with a value.

Created using curly braces ({}) with key-value pairs separated by commas (e.g., {'name': 'John', 'age': 30}).

Set: Unordered collection of unique items.

Created using curly braces ({}) or the set() function (e.g., {1, 2, 3}, set([1, 2, 3])).

```
# Variables and Data Types
age = 25    # int
height = 5.9    # float
name = 'John'    # string
is_student = True    # boolean

# Lists
numbers = [1, 2, 3, 4, 5]    # list
fruits = ['apple', 'banana', 'orange']    # list

# Tuple
coordinates = (10, 20)    # tuple

# Dictionary
person = {'name': 'Alice', 'age': 30}    # dictionary

# Set
unique_numbers = {1, 2, 3, 4, 5}    # set
```

Control Flow

If Statements: if statement: It allows you to execute a block of code if a specified condition is true.

elif (else if) statement: It allows you to check multiple conditions after the initial if statement. It is executed if the preceding conditions are false and its condition is true.

else statement: It is executed if none of the preceding conditions are true.

Syntax:

```
if condition:
    # Code block to execute if condition is true
elif condition:
    # Code block to execute if condition is true
else:
    # Code block to execute if none of the above
conditions are true
```

Example:

```
# Example of if statement
age = 18
if age >= 18:
    print("You are an adult")
else:
    print("You are a minor")
```

Loops:

for loop: It iterates over a sequence (e.g., list, tuple, string) and executes a block of code for each item in the sequence.

while loop: It repeats a block of code as long as a specified condition is true.

Syntax:

```python
# For loop
for item in sequence:
    # Code block to execute for each item in the sequence

# While loop
while condition:
    # Code block to execute as long as the condition is true
```

Example:

```python
# Example of for loop
fruits = ['apple', 'banana', 'orange']
for fruit in fruits:
    print(fruit)

# Example of while loop
num = 1
while num <= 5:
    print(num)
    num += 1
```

Functions and recursion

Defining Functions: Functions in Python are defined using the **def** keyword, followed by the function name and parentheses containing optional parameters.

The body of the function is indented and contains the code to be executed when the function is called.

Syntax:

```
def function_name(parameters):
    # Function body
    # Code to execute
    return value
```

Example:

```
# Function definition
def greet(name):
    return "Hello, " + name + "!"

# Function call
message = greet("Alice")
print(message)  # Output: Hello, Alice!
```

Parameters and Arguments:

Parameters are variables that are listed in the function definition. Arguments are the values passed into the function when it is called.

Example:

```
# Function definition with parameters
def add(a, b):
    return a + b
```

```python
# Function call with arguments
result = add(3, 5)
print(result)  # Output: 8
```

Return Statement:

The return statement is used to exit a function and return a value to the caller.

Example:

```python
def multiply(a, b):
    return a * b

result = multiply(4, 6)
print(result)  # Output: 24
```

Recursion:

What is Recursion?
Recursion is a technique in which a function calls itself to solve smaller instances of the same problem.

Recursion consists of two main parts: base case(s) and recursive case(s).

Example:

```python
def factorial(n):
    if n == 0:
        return 1  # Base case
    else:
        return n * factorial(n - 1)  # Recursive case

result = factorial(5)
print(result)  # Output: 120 (5 * 4 * 3 * 2 * 1)
```

In the above example, **factorial()** is a recursive function that calculates the factorial of a number. It calls itself with a smaller value **(n - 1)** until it reaches the base case **(n == 0)**.

Exception Handling

Try-Except Block: The try-except block is used to handle exceptions (errors) that occur during the execution of a block of code.

The code within the try block is executed. If an exception occurs, the control immediately moves to the corresponding except block.

Syntax:

```
try:
    # Code that may raise an exception
except ExceptionName:
    # Code to handle the exception
```

Example:

```
try:
    num = int(input("Enter a number: "))
    result = 10 / num
    print("Result:", result)
except ZeroDivisionError:
    print("Error: Cannot divide by zero")
except ValueError:
    print("Error: Invalid input. Please enter a valid number")
```

Multiple Except Blocks: You can have multiple except blocks to handle different types of exceptions separately.

Generic Except Block: You can use a generic except block to catch any exception that is not handled by the specific except blocks.

Example:
```
try:
    # Code that may raise an exception
except ValueError:
```

```
    # Code to handle ValueError
except ZeroDivisionError:
    # Code to handle ZeroDivisionError
except:
    # Code to handle any other exception
```

Finally Block: The finally block is optional and is used to execute code regardless of whether an exception occurs or not. It is often used for cleanup operations (e.g., closing files, releasing resources).

Example:

```
try:
    # Code that may raise an exception
except ExceptionName:
    # Code to handle the exception
finally:
    # Code that always executes, regardless of exceptions
```

Custom Exceptions: You can define custom exception classes by subclassing the built-in Exception class. This allows you to create your own exception types to handle specific error conditions in your code.

Example:

```
class MyCustomError(Exception):
    pass

try:
    # Code that may raise MyCustomError
except MyCustomError:
    # Code to handle MyCustomError
```

Basic Data Structures

Lists

Creating Lists: Lists are created by enclosing comma-separated values within square brackets [ ].

Syntax:

```
# Empty list
empty_list = []

# List with elements
my_list = [1, 2, 3, 'apple', 'banana', True]
```

Accessing Elements:

Elements in a list are accessed using index notation. Indices start from 0 for the first element and -1 for the last element.

You can also use slicing to extract a sublist from a list.

Example:

```
my_list = [10, 20, 30, 40, 50]

# Accessing individual elements
print(my_list[0])    # Output: 10
print(my_list[-1])   # Output: 50

# Slicing
print(my_list[1:4])  # Output: [20, 30, 40]
```

Modifying Lists:

Lists are mutable, meaning you can change their elements after creation.

You can modify individual elements, append new elements, insert elements at specific positions, remove elements, and more.

Example:

```python
my_list = [1, 2, 3]

# Modifying elements
my_list[1] = 10   # Update the second element
print(my_list)    # Output: [1, 10, 3]

# Appending elements
my_list.append(4)   # Append 4 to the end
print(my_list)      # Output: [1, 10, 3, 4]

# Inserting elements
my_list.insert(1, 5)   # Insert 5 at index 1
print(my_list)         # Output: [1, 5, 10, 3, 4]

# Removing elements
my_list.remove(3)   # Remove the first occurrence of 3
print(my_list)      # Output: [1, 5, 10, 4]
```

List Operations:

Lists support various operations such as concatenation (+), repetition (*), membership (in), and length (len()).

Example:

```python
list1 = [1, 2, 3]
list2 = [4, 5, 6]

# Concatenation
result = list1 + list2   # Output: [1, 2, 3, 4, 5, 6]

# Repetition
result = list1 * 3   # Output: [1, 2, 3, 1, 2, 3, 1, 2, 3]

# Membership
print(2 in list1)   # Output: True
```

```python
# Length
print(len(list1))   # Output: 3
```

List Comprehension: List comprehensions provide a concise way to create lists based on existing lists or other iterable objects.

Example:

```python
# List comprehension to generate squares of numbers from 1 to 5
squares = [x ** 2 for x in range(1, 6)]
print(squares)   # Output: [1, 4, 9, 16, 25]
```

Tuples

Tuples are another fundamental data structure in Python, similar to lists but with some key differences. Tuples are immutable, ordered collections of items, meaning once they are created, their elements cannot be changed, added, or removed.

Here's an overview of tuples in Python:

Tuples:

Creating Tuples:
Tuples are created by enclosing comma-separated values within parentheses ().

Syntax:

```
# Empty tuple
empty_tuple = ()

# Tuple with elements
my_tuple = (1, 2, 3, 'apple', 'banana')
```

Accessing Elements:

Elements in a tuple are accessed using index notation, similar to lists.

Example:

```
my_tuple = (10, 20, 30, 40, 50)

# Accessing individual elements
print(my_tuple[0])   # Output: 10
print(my_tuple[-1])  # Output: 50
```

Tuple Unpacking:

Tuple unpacking allows you to assign the elements of a tuple to individual variables.

Example:

```
my_tuple = (1, 2, 3)
x, y, z = my_tuple
print(x, y, z)   # Output: 1 2 3
```

Immutable Nature:
Unlike lists, tuples are immutable, meaning you cannot modify their elements after creation.

Example:

```
my_tuple = (1, 2, 3)
my_tuple[0] = 10   # Error: 'tuple' object does not support item assignment
```

Tuple Operations:

Tuples support various operations such as concatenation (+), repetition (*), membership (in), and length (len()).

Example:

```
tuple1 = (1, 2, 3)
tuple2 = (4, 5, 6)

# Concatenation
result = tuple1 + tuple2   # Output: (1, 2, 3, 4, 5, 6)

# Repetition
result = tuple1 * 3   # Output: (1, 2, 3, 1, 2, 3, 1, 2, 3)

# Membership
print(2 in tuple1)   # Output: True

# Length
print(len(tuple1))   # Output: 3
```

Uses of Tuples:

Tuples are commonly used to represent fixed collections of items, such as coordinates, database records, and function return values. They are often used in situations where immutability and the fixed order of elements are desired characteristics.

Dictionaries

Dictionaries are another essential data structure in Python, providing a way to store and retrieve data in the form of key-value pairs. Unlike sequences such as lists and tuples, which are indexed by a range of numbers, dictionaries are indexed by keys, which can be of various data types.

Here's an overview of dictionaries in Python:

Dictionaries:

Creating Dictionaries:

Dictionaries are created by enclosing comma-separated key-value pairs within curly braces {}.

Syntax:

```
# Empty dictionary
empty_dict = {}

# Dictionary with elements
my_dict = {'name': 'John', 'age': 30, 'city': 'New York'}
```

Accessing Elements:

Elements in a dictionary are accessed using keys instead of indices.

Example:

```python
my_dict = {'name': 'John', 'age': 30, 'city': 'New York'}

# Accessing individual elements
print(my_dict['name'])   # Output: John
print(my_dict['age'])    # Output: 30
```

Modifying Dictionaries:

Dictionaries are mutable, meaning you can add, modify, or remove key-value pairs after creation.

Example:

```python
my_dict = {'name': 'John', 'age': 30, 'city': 'New York'}

# Modifying elements
my_dict['age'] = 35  # Update the value of 'age'
print(my_dict)  # Output: {'name': 'John', 'age': 35, 'city': 'New York'}

# Adding new elements
my_dict['gender'] = 'Male'
print(my_dict)  # Output: {'name': 'John', 'age': 35, 'city': 'New York', 'gender': 'Male'}

# Removing elements
del my_dict['city']
print(my_dict)  # Output: {'name': 'John', 'age': 35, 'gender': 'Male'}
```

Dictionary Operations:

Dictionaries support various operations such as membership (in), length (len()), and iteration over keys, values, or key-value pairs.

Example:

```python
my_dict = {'name': 'John', 'age': 30, 'city': 'New York'}

# Membership
print('age' in my_dict)   # Output: True

# Length
print(len(my_dict))  # Output: 3

# Iteration over keys
for key in my_dict:
    print(key)

# Iteration over values
for value in my_dict.values():
    print(value)

# Iteration over key-value pairs
for key, value in my_dict.items():
    print(key, value)
```

Uses of Dictionaries:

- Dictionaries are commonly used to represent mappings between keys and values, such as database records, configuration settings, and JSON data.

- They are suitable for situations where fast and efficient lookup of values based on keys is required.

Sets

Creating Sets:

Sets are created by enclosing comma-separated elements within curly braces {}.

Syntax:

```
# Empty set (Note: Cannot be created using {})
empty_set = set()

# Set with elements
my_set = {1, 2, 3, 4, 5}
```
Accessing Elements:

Elements in a set cannot be accessed using indices because sets are unordered collections. However, you can check for membership using the in operator.

Example:

```
my_set = {1, 2, 3, 4, 5}

# Checking for membership
print(3 in my_set)   # Output: True
```

Modifying Sets:

Sets are mutable, meaning you can add and remove elements after creation.

However, sets do not support indexing and slicing operations.

Example:

```
my_set = {1, 2, 3}

# Adding elements
my_set.add(4)
```

```python
print(my_set)   # Output: {1, 2, 3, 4}

# Removing elements
my_set.remove(2)
print(my_set)   # Output: {1, 3, 4}
```

Set Operations:

Sets support various mathematical operations such as union, intersection, difference, and symmetric difference.

Example:

```python
set1 = {1, 2, 3}
set2 = {3, 4, 5}

# Union
union_set = set1 | set2   # or set1.union(set2)
print(union_set)   # Output: {1, 2, 3, 4, 5}

# Intersection
intersection_set = set1 & set2   # or
set1.intersection(set2)
print(intersection_set)   # Output: {3}

# Difference
difference_set = set1 - set2   # or set1.difference(set2)
print(difference_set)   # Output: {1, 2}

# Symmetric Difference
symmetric_difference_set = set1 ^ set2   # or
set1.symmetric_difference(set2)
print(symmetric_difference_set)   # Output: {1, 2, 4, 5}
```

Uses of Sets:

- Sets are useful for eliminating duplicate elements from a collection and performing fast membership tests.

- They are often used in situations where you need to perform mathematical operations on collections of unique elements.

Elementary Algorithms

Sorting Algorithms

Bubble Sort: Bubble sort is a basic sorting algorithm that repeatedly steps through the list, compares adjacent elements, and swaps them if they are in the wrong order.

The pass through the list is repeated until the list is sorted.

It's called "bubble" sort because with each pass, the larger elements "bubble" to the top of the list.

The algorithm has a time complexity of $O(n^2)$, making it inefficient for large lists, but it's easy to understand and implement.

Example:

```python
def bubble_sort(arr):
    n = len(arr)
    # Traverse through all array elements
    for i in range(n):
        # Last i elements are already in place
        for j in range(0, n - i - 1):
            # Traverse the array from 0 to n-i-1
            # Swap if the element found is greater than the next element
            if arr[j] > arr[j + 1]:
                arr[j], arr[j + 1] = arr[j + 1], arr[j]

# Example usage
array = [64, 34, 25, 12, 22, 11, 90]
bubble_sort(array)
print("Sorted array using Bubble Sort:", array)
```

Selection Sort: Selection sort is another simple sorting algorithm that divides the input list into two parts: a sorted sublist and an unsorted sublist.

Initially, the sorted sublist is empty, and the unsorted sublist contains all elements.

The algorithm finds the smallest (or largest, depending on sorting order) element in the unsorted sublist and swaps it with the leftmost unsorted element.

After each iteration, the sorted sublist grows, and the unsorted sublist shrinks until no elements remain.

Selection sort has a time complexity of $O(n^2)$, similar to bubble sort, but it typically performs fewer swaps.

Both of these sorting algorithms are considered elementary because they are straightforward and easy to understand, although they may not be the most efficient for large datasets. They are often used for educational purposes or for sorting small datasets where simplicity is valued over performance.

Example:

```python
def selection_sort(arr):
    n = len(arr)
    # Traverse through all array elements
    for i in range(n):
        # Find the minimum element in the remaining unsorted array
        min_idx = i
        for j in range(i + 1, n):
            if arr[j] < arr[min_idx]:
                min_idx = j
        # Swap the found minimum element with the first element
        arr[i], arr[min_idx] = arr[min_idx], arr[i]

# Example usage
array = [64, 34, 25, 12, 22, 11, 90]
```

```
selection_sort(array)
print("Sorted array using Selection Sort:", array)
```

Searching algorithms

Searching algorithms are used to find the presence or absence of a target value within a collection of data. Here are two commonly used searching algorithms:

Linear Search: Linear search is a simple searching algorithm that sequentially checks each element in a collection until the target value is found or all elements have been checked.

It works well for small datasets or unsorted collections.

The time complexity of linear search is O(n) in the worst-case scenario, where n is the number of elements in the collection.

Example:

```
def linear_search(arr, target):
    for i in range(len(arr)):
        if arr[i] == target:
            return i    # Return the index of the target if found
    return -1    # Return -1 if the target is not found

# Example usage
array = [4, 2, 7, 1, 9, 5]
target = 7
result = linear_search(array, target)
if result != -1:
    print(f"Element {target} is present at index {result}")
else:
    print(f"Element {target} is not present in the array")
```

Binary Search: Binary search is a more efficient searching algorithm applicable only to sorted collections.

It works by repeatedly dividing the sorted collection in half and comparing the target value with the middle element.

If the target value matches the middle element, the search is successful.
If the target value is less than the middle element, the search continues on the lower half of the collection; otherwise, it continues on the upper half.

Binary search has a time complexity of $O(\log n)$, making it significantly faster than linear search for large datasets.

Example:

```python
def binary_search(arr, target):
    low = 0
    high = len(arr) - 1
    while low <= high:
        mid = (low + high) // 2
        if arr[mid] == target:
            return mid  # Return the index of the target if found
        elif arr[mid] < target:
            low = mid + 1
        else:
            high = mid - 1
    return -1  # Return -1 if the target is not found

# Example usage
sorted_array = [1, 2, 3, 4, 5, 6, 7, 8, 9]
target = 7
result = binary_search(sorted_array, target)
if result != -1:
    print(f"Element {target} is present at index {result}")
else:
    print(f"Element {target} is not present in the array")
```

Mathematical Algorithms:

Factorial: Calculates the factorial of a non-negative integer n, denoted by n!, which is the product of all positive integers less than or equal to n.

Example:
```
def factorial(n):
    if n == 0:
        return 1
    else:
        return n * factorial(n-1)

# Example usage:
n = 5
print("Factorial of", n, "is", factorial(n))
```

Fibonacci Sequence: Generates the Fibonacci sequence up to the nth term, where each term is the sum of the two preceding terms.

Example:

```
def fibonacci(n):
    if n <= 1:
        return n
    else:
        return fibonacci(n-1) + fibonacci(n-2)

# Example usage:
n = 7
print("Fibonacci sequence up to", n, "terms:")
for i in range(n):
    print(fibonacci(i), end=" ")
```

String Algorithms:

Reverse a String: Reverses a given string s by slicing it with a step of -1.

Example:
```
def reverse_string(s):
    return s[::-1]

# Example usage:
s = "hello"
print("Original:", s)
print("Reversed:", reverse_string(s))
```

Check Palindrome: Determines whether a given string s is a palindrome, which reads the same forwards and backwards.

Example:

```
def is_palindrome(s):
    return s == s[::-1]

# Example usage:
s = "radar"
print("Is", s, "a palindrome?", is_palindrome(s))
```

Recursion:

Sum of Digits: Computes the sum of digits of a non-negative integer n using recursion.

Example:

```
def sum_of_digits(n):
    if n == 0:
        return 0
    else:
        return n % 10 + sum_of_digits(n // 10)

# Example usage:
n = 12345
print("Sum of digits in", n, "is", sum_of_digits(n))
```

Greatest Common Divisor (GCD): Finds the greatest common divisor of two non-negative integers a and b using the Euclidean algorithm and recursion.

Example:

```
def gcd(a, b):
    if b == 0:
        return a
    else:
        return gcd(b, a % b)

# Example usage:
a, b = 36, 24
print("GCD of", a, "and", b, "is", gcd(a, b))
```

Introduction to Data Structures

Data structures are a fundamental concept in computer science that enable efficient organization, storage, and manipulation of data. They provide a way to represent and manage collections of data in a structured manner, allowing for optimized access, insertion, deletion, and searching operations.

Here's an overview of some common data structures:

- **Stack**
- **Queue**
- **Linked List**

Stack

A stack is a fundamental data structure that follows the Last In, First Out (LIFO) principle. It is named "stack" because it resembles a stack of plates, where you can only add or remove plates from the top.

Here are some key features and operations of a stack:

Features:

- A stack is a collection of elements with two main operations: push and pop.
- Elements are added or removed from the top of the stack.
- Stacks are often implemented using arrays or linked lists.

Operations:

- **Push:** Adds an element to the top of the stack.
- **Pop:** Removes and returns the top element from the stack.
- **Peek (or Top):** Returns the top element of the stack without removing it.
- **isEmpty:** Checks if the stack is empty.
- **Size:** Returns the number of elements in the stack.

Applications:

- Stacks are commonly used in programming languages for function call management and maintaining the call stack.

- They are used in expression evaluation algorithms (e.g., infix to postfix conversion, postfix evaluation).

- Undo functionality in text editors and command-line interfaces often uses stacks to keep track of previous states or commands.

- Backtracking algorithms and depth-first search (DFS) traversal utilize stacks to keep track of visited nodes or search paths.

Implementation:

- Stacks can be implemented using arrays or linked lists.

- Array-based implementations are simpler and provide constant-time access to the top element, but may require resizing if the stack grows beyond its initial capacity.

- Linked list-based implementations allow for dynamic memory allocation and efficient resizing, but may have slightly higher overhead due to pointer manipulation.

Here's a simple implementation of a stack in Python using a list:

```
class Stack:
```

```python
def __init__(self):
    self.items = []

def isEmpty(self):
    return len(self.items) == 0

def push(self, item):
    self.items.append(item)

def pop(self):
    if not self.isEmpty():
        return self.items.pop()
    else:
        raise IndexError("Stack is empty")

def peek(self):
    if not self.isEmpty():
        return self.items[-1]
    else:
        raise IndexError("Stack is empty")

def size(self):
    return len(self.items)
```

In this implementation, push() adds an element to the top of the stack, pop() removes and returns the top element, peek() returns the top element without removing it, isEmpty() checks if the stack is empty, and size() returns the number of elements in the stack.

Queue

A queue is another fundamental data structure that follows the First In, First Out (FIFO) principle. It is similar to a line of people waiting to be served, where the person who has been waiting the longest is served first.

Here are some key features and operations of a queue:

Features:

- A queue is a collection of elements with two main operations: enqueue and dequeue.
- Elements are added to the rear (enqueue) and removed from the front (dequeue) of the queue.
- Queues are often implemented using arrays or linked lists.

Operations:

- **Enqueue:** Adds an element to the rear of the queue.
- **Dequeue:** Removes and returns the element from the front of the queue.
- **Front:** Returns the front element of the queue without removing it.
- **isEmpty:** Checks if the queue is empty.

- **Size:** Returns the number of elements in the queue.

Applications:

- Queues are commonly used in scheduling algorithms, such as job scheduling in operating systems.
- They are used in breadth-first search (BFS) traversal algorithms for graph traversal.
- Print queues in computer systems use queues to manage the order of print jobs.
- Buffer management in networking and I/O systems often employs queues to manage data flow.

Implementation:

- Queues can be implemented using arrays or linked lists.
- Array-based implementations are simple and provide constant-time access to both the front and rear of the queue, but may require resizing if the queue grows beyond its initial capacity.

- Linked list-based implementations allow for dynamic memory allocation and efficient resizing, but may have slightly higher overhead due to pointer manipulation.

Here's a simple implementation of a queue in Python using a list:

```
class Queue:
    def __init__(self):
        self.items = []

    def isEmpty(self):
        return len(self.items) == 0

    def enqueue(self, item):
        self.items.append(item)

    def dequeue(self):
        if not self.isEmpty():
            return self.items.pop(0)
        else:
            raise IndexError("Queue is empty")

    def front(self):
        if not self.isEmpty():
            return self.items[0]
        else:
            raise IndexError("Queue is empty")

    def size(self):
        return len(self.items)
```

In this implementation, enqueue() adds an element to the rear of the queue, dequeue() removes and returns the element from the front of the queue, front() returns the front element without removing it, isEmpty() checks if the queue is empty, and size() returns the number of elements in the queue.

Linked List

A linked list is a linear data structure where elements are stored in memory as separate objects called nodes. Each node contains both data and a reference (or pointer) to the next node in the sequence. Unlike arrays, linked lists do not require contiguous memory allocation, allowing for dynamic memory allocation and efficient insertion and deletion operations.

Here are some key features and operations of a linked list:

Features:

- A linked list consists of nodes, where each node contains data and a reference to the next node in the sequence.
- The last node in the list typically points to None, indicating the end of the list.
- Linked lists can be singly linked (each node points to the next node) or doubly linked (each node points to both the next and previous nodes).

Operations:

Insertion:

- **At the beginning:** Insert a new node at the beginning of the list.

- **At the end:** Insert a new node at the end of the list.
- **In the middle:** Insert a new node at a specific position in the list.

Deletion:

- **At the beginning:** Remove the first node from the list.
- **At the end:** Remove the last node from the list.
- **In the middle:** Remove a node from a specific position in the list.
- **Traversal:** Traverse the list to access or modify each node's data.
- **Search:** Search for a specific value in the list.

Types of Linked Lists:

- **Singly Linked List:** Each node has a reference to the next node in the sequence.
- **Doubly Linked List:** Each node has references to both the next and previous nodes in the sequence.
- **Circular Linked List**: The last node in the list points back to the first node, forming a circular structure.

Applications:

- Linked lists are often used when the size of the data structure is not known in advance or when frequent insertions and deletions are required.

- They are used in various applications, such as implementing stacks, queues, hash tables, and adjacency lists for graphs.

Implementation:

- Linked lists can be implemented using classes and pointers (references) in languages like Python, Java, C++, and others.

- Each node in the linked list contains two fields: one for data and another for the reference to the next node.

Here's a simple implementation of a singly linked list in Python:

```python
class Node:
    def __init__(self, data):
        self.data = data
        self.next = None

class LinkedList:
    def __init__(self):
        self.head = None

    def insert_at_beginning(self, data):
        new_node = Node(data)
        new_node.next = self.head
        self.head = new_node
```

```python
    def insert_at_end(self, data):
        new_node = Node(data)
        if self.head is None:
            self.head = new_node
            return
        last_node = self.head
        while last_node.next:
            last_node = last_node.next
        last_node.next = new_node

    def display(self):
        current = self.head
        while current:
            print(current.data, end=" ")
            current = current.next
        print()

# Example usage:
ll = LinkedList()
ll.insert_at_beginning(1)
ll.insert_at_end(2)
ll.insert_at_end(3)
ll.display()   # Output: 1 2 3
```

In this implementation, each node of the linked list is represented using the Node class, and the linked list itself is represented using the **LinkedList** class. You can insert nodes at the beginning or end of the list and display the contents of the list.

More Data Structures

Hash table

A hash table (hash map) is a data structure that stores key-value pairs and provides efficient insertion, deletion, and lookup operations.

It uses a hash function to compute an index (hash code) for each key, allowing for constant-time access to values associated with keys.

Hash tables are widely used in applications such as implementing associative arrays, symbol tables, and caching.

```python
class HashTable:
    def __init__(self, size):
        self.size = size
        self.table = [[] for _ in range(size)]

    def _hash(self, key):
        return hash(key) % self.size

    def insert(self, key, value):
        index = self._hash(key)
        for pair in self.table[index]:
            if pair[0] == key:
                pair[1] = value  # Update existing key
                return
        self.table[index].append([key, value])  # Add new key-value pair

    def get(self, key):
        index = self._hash(key)
        for pair in self.table[index]:
            if pair[0] == key:
                return pair[1]  # Return value associated with key
        return None  # Key not found

    def remove(self, key):
        index = self._hash(key)
```

```python
        for i, pair in enumerate(self.table[index]):
            if pair[0] == key:
                del self.table[index][i]  # Remove key-value pair
                return
        raise KeyError(f'Key "{key}" not found')

# Example usage:
hash_table = HashTable(10)
hash_table.insert('apple', 5)
hash_table.insert('banana', 10)
hash_table.insert('orange', 15)

print("Value for key 'apple':", hash_table.get('apple'))  # Output: 5
print("Value for key 'banana':", hash_table.get('banana'))  # Output: 10
print("Value for key 'orange':", hash_table.get('orange'))  # Output: 15

hash_table.insert('apple', 7)  # Update value for existing key
print("Updated value for key 'apple':", hash_table.get('apple'))  # Output: 7

hash_table.remove('banana')
print("Value for key 'banana' after removal:", hash_table.get('banana'))  # Output: None
```

Trees

Binary tree: A binary tree is a hierarchical data structure consisting of nodes, where each node has at most two children: a left child and a right child.

It is recursively defined and can be used to represent hierarchical relationships, such as family trees, file systems, and expression trees.

Common operations on binary trees include insertion, deletion, traversal (in-order, pre-order, post-order), and searching.

Example:

```python
class TreeNode:
    def __init__(self, value):
        self.value = value
        self.left = None
        self.right = None

class BinaryTree:
    def __init__(self):
        self.root = None

    def insert(self, value):
        if not self.root:
            self.root = TreeNode(value)
        else:
            self._insert_recursively(self.root, value)

    def _insert_recursively(self, node, value):
```

```python
            if value < node.value:
                if not node.left:
                    node.left = TreeNode(value)
                else:
                    self._insert_recursively(node.left, value)
            elif value > node.value:
                if not node.right:
                    node.right = TreeNode(value)
                else:
                    self._insert_recursively(node.right, value)

    def in_order_traversal(self):
        result = []
        self._in_order_traversal_recursively(self.root, result)
        return result

    def _in_order_traversal_recursively(self, node, result):
        if node:
            self._in_order_traversal_recursively(node.left, result)
            result.append(node.value)
            self._in_order_traversal_recursively(node.right, result)

# Example usage:
tree = BinaryTree()
tree.insert(5)
tree.insert(3)
tree.insert(8)
tree.insert(2)
tree.insert(4)
tree.insert(7)
tree.insert(9)
```

```
print("In-order traversal:", tree.in_order_traversal())
# Output: [2, 3, 4, 5, 7, 8, 9]
```

Binary search tree: A binary search tree is a binary tree in which the value of each node is greater than all values in its left subtree and less than all values in its right subtree.

BSTs support efficient searching, insertion, and deletion operations, with average time complexity of O(log n) for each operation.

They are commonly used in applications such as database indexing, implementing sets and maps, and maintaining sorted sequences.

Example:
```
class TreeNode:
    def __init__(self, value):
        self.value = value
        self.left = None
        self.right = None

class BST:
    def __init__(self):
        self.root = None

    def insert(self, value):
        if not self.root:
            self.root = TreeNode(value)
        else:
            self._insert_recursively(self.root, value)
```

```python
    def _insert_recursively(self, node, value):
        if value < node.value:
            if not node.left:
                node.left = TreeNode(value)
            else:
                self._insert_recursively(node.left, value)
        elif value > node.value:
            if not node.right:
                node.right = TreeNode(value)
            else:
                self._insert_recursively(node.right, value)
        # Ignore if the value already exists in the BST

    def search(self, value):
        return self._search_recursively(self.root, value)

    def _search_recursively(self, node, value):
        if not node:
            return False
        if node.value == value:
            return True
        elif value < node.value:
            return self._search_recursively(node.left, value)
        else:
            return self._search_recursively(node.right, value)

# Example usage:
bst = BST()
bst.insert(5)
bst.insert(3)
bst.insert(8)
bst.insert(2)
```

```python
bst.insert(4)
bst.insert(7)
bst.insert(9)

print("Search for value 4:", bst.search(4))  # Output: True
print("Search for value 6:", bst.search(6))  # Output: False
```

Graphs

A graph is a non-linear data structure consisting of vertices (nodes) connected by edges (links).

It is used to model relationships between objects and entities in various domains, such as social networks, transportation networks, and computer networks.

Graphs can be directed (edges have a specific direction) or undirected (edges have no direction) and may contain cycles or be acyclic.

Common graph algorithms include depth-first search (DFS), breadth-first search (BFS), shortest path algorithms (e.g., Dijkstra's algorithm), and minimum spanning tree algorithms (e.g., Prim's algorithm, Kruskal's algorithm).

Here's a Python implementation of an undirected graph along with an example:

```python
class Graph:
    def __init__(self):
        self.vertices = {}

    def add_vertex(self, vertex):
        if vertex not in self.vertices:
            self.vertices[vertex] = []

    def add_edge(self, vertex1, vertex2):
        if vertex1 in self.vertices and vertex2 in self.vertices:
            self.vertices[vertex1].append(vertex2)
            self.vertices[vertex2].append(vertex1)

    def __str__(self):
        return f"Graph: {self.vertices}"

# Example usage:
```

```
g = Graph()
g.add_vertex('A')
g.add_vertex('B')
g.add_vertex('C')
g.add_vertex('D')

g.add_edge('A', 'B')
g.add_edge('A', 'C')
g.add_edge('B', 'C')
g.add_edge('B', 'D')

print(g)

# Output:

# Graph: {'A': ['B', 'C'], 'B': ['A', 'C', 'D'], 'C': ['A', 'B'], 'D': ['B']}
```

Practical Applications

Problem-solving strategies

Dynamic Programming: Used in optimization problems where solutions can be efficiently obtained by breaking them down into simpler subproblems. Examples include the knapsack problem, longest common subsequence, and Fibonacci sequence computation.

Knapsack problem: The knapsack problem is a classic optimization problem in computer science. There are several variations of the knapsack problem, but one common version is the 0/1 knapsack problem, which is described as follows:

Given a set of items, each with a weight and a value, determine the number of each item to include in a knapsack so that the total weight is less than or equal to a given limit, and the total value is maximized.

Here's a Python implementation of the 0/1 knapsack problem using dynamic programming:

```python
def knapsack(weights, values, capacity):
    n = len(weights)
    dp = [[0] * (capacity + 1) for _ in range(n + 1)]

    for i in range(1, n + 1):
        for j in range(1, capacity + 1):
            if weights[i - 1] <= j:
                dp[i][j] = max(dp[i - 1][j], values[i - 1] + dp[i - 1][j - weights[i - 1]])
            else:
                dp[i][j] = dp[i - 1][j]

    # Reconstructing the solution
    selected_items = []
    i, j = n, capacity
    while i > 0 and j > 0:
        if dp[i][j] != dp[i - 1][j]:
            selected_items.append(i - 1)
            j -= weights[i - 1]
        i -= 1
```

```
        return dp[n][capacity], selected_items

# Example usage:
weights = [2, 3, 4, 5]
values = [3, 4, 5, 6]
capacity = 8
max_value, selected_items = knapsack(weights, values, capacity)
print("Maximum value:", max_value)
print("Selected items:", selected_items)
```

In this example, weights and values represent the weights and values of the items respectively, and capacity represents the maximum weight that the knapsack can hold. The knapsack function returns the maximum value that can be achieved and the indices of the selected items.

The Longest Common Subsequence: (LCS) problem is a classic problem in dynamic programming where the task is to find the longest subsequence that is present in both of the given sequences.

Here's a Python implementation of the LCS problem using dynamic programming:

```
def longest_common_subsequence(X, Y):
    m = len(X)
    n = len(Y)

    # Create a table to store lengths of LCSs
    dp = [[0] * (n + 1) for _ in range(m + 1)]

    # Building the dp table in a bottom-up manner
    for i in range(1, m + 1):
        for j in range(1, n + 1):
            if X[i - 1] == Y[j - 1]:
                dp[i][j] = dp[i - 1][j - 1] + 1
            else:
```

```
            dp[i][j] = max(dp[i - 1][j], dp[i][j - 1])

    # Finding the LCS from the dp table
    lcs = ""
    i, j = m, n
    while i > 0 and j > 0:
        if X[i - 1] == Y[j - 1]:
            lcs = X[i - 1] + lcs
            i -= 1
            j -= 1
        elif dp[i - 1][j] > dp[i][j - 1]:
            i -= 1
        else:
            j -= 1

    return lcs

# Example usage:
X = "ABCBDAB"
Y = "BDCAB"
print("Longest Common Subsequence:", longest_common_subsequence(X, Y))
```

In this implementation, the longest_common_subsequence function takes two strings X and Y as input and returns the longest common subsequence between them. The function builds a dynamic programming table dp to store the lengths of LCSs of different prefixes of X and Y, and then uses the table to reconstruct the LCS itself.

The Fibonacci sequence: is a series of numbers where each number is the sum of the two preceding ones, usually starting with 0 and 1. Here's a Python implementation of computing the Fibonacci sequence using both iterative and recursive approaches:

Iterative approach:

```
def fibonacci_iterative(n):
    fib = [0, 1]
```

```
    for i in range(2, n + 1):
        fib.append(fib[i - 1] + fib[i - 2])
    return fib[n]
```

```
# Example usage:
n = 10
print("Fibonacci number at index", n, ":",
fibonacci_iterative(n))
```

Recursive approach:

```
def fibonacci_recursive(n):
    if n <= 1:
        return n
    else:
        return fibonacci_recursive(n - 1) +
fibonacci_recursive(n - 2)
```

```
# Example usage:
n = 10
print("Fibonacci number at index", n, ":",
fibonacci_recursive(n))
```

While the iterative approach is more efficient in terms of time complexity, the recursive approach is simpler to implement. However, the recursive approach may lead to stack overflow errors for large values of n due to its exponential time complexity. Therefore, for larger values of n, it's recommended to use the iterative approach.

Greedy Algorithms:
Offer simple, intuitive solutions by making locally optimal choices at each step. Applications include minimum spanning tree algorithms (e.g., Prim's and Kruskal's algorithms), Huffman coding for data compression, and Dijkstra's algorithm for shortest paths.

Prim's and Kruskal's algorithms are two popular algorithms used to find the minimum spanning tree (MST) of a connected, undirected graph with weighted edges. Here are Python implementations of both algorithms:

Prim's Algorithm:

```python
import heapq

def prim(graph):
    n = len(graph)
    visited = [False] * n
    min_heap = [(0, 0)]  # (weight, vertex)
    mst_cost = 0

    while min_heap:
        weight, u = heapq.heappop(min_heap)
        if not visited[u]:
            visited[u] = True
            mst_cost += weight
            for v, w in graph[u]:
                if not visited[v]:
                    heapq.heappush(min_heap, (w, v))

    return mst_cost

# Example usage:
graph = {
    0: [(1, 2), (2, 1)],
    1: [(0, 2), (2, 3), (3, 5)],
    2: [(0, 1), (1, 3)],
    3: [(1, 5), (2, 3)]
}
print("Minimum Spanning Tree cost (Prim's Algorithm):", prim(graph))
```

Kruskal's Algorithm:

```python
class UnionFind:
    def __init__(self, n):
        self.parent = list(range(n))
        self.rank = [0] * n

    def find(self, x):
```

```python
            if self.parent[x] != x:
                self.parent[x] = self.find(self.parent[x])
            return self.parent[x]

        def union(self, x, y):
            root_x = self.find(x)
            root_y = self.find(y)
            if root_x != root_y:
                if self.rank[root_x] < self.rank[root_y]:
                    self.parent[root_x] = root_y
                elif self.rank[root_x] > self.rank[root_y]:
                    self.parent[root_y] = root_x
                else:
                    self.parent[root_y] = root_x
                    self.rank[root_x] += 1

def kruskal(graph):
    n = len(graph)
    edges = [(weight, u, v) for u in range(n) for v, weight in graph[u]]
    edges.sort()
    uf = UnionFind(n)
    mst_cost = 0

    for weight, u, v in edges:
        if uf.find(u) != uf.find(v):
            uf.union(u, v)
            mst_cost += weight

    return mst_cost

# Example usage:
graph = {
    0: [(1, 2), (2, 1)],
    1: [(0, 2), (2, 3), (3, 5)],
    2: [(0, 1), (1, 3)],
    3: [(1, 5), (2, 3)]
}
```

```
print("Minimum Spanning Tree cost (Kruskal's 
Algorithm):", kruskal(graph))
```

Divide and Conquer: Breaks down a problem into smaller, more manageable subproblems, solves them independently, and then combines their solutions to obtain the final result. Examples include merge sort, quicksort, and binary search.

Merge sort:

```
def merge_sort(arr):
    if len(arr) > 1:
        mid = len(arr) // 2
        left_half = arr[:mid]
        right_half = arr[mid:]

        merge_sort(left_half)
        merge_sort(right_half)

        i = j = k = 0

        while i < len(left_half) and j < len(right_half):
            if left_half[i] < right_half[j]:
                arr[k] = left_half[i]
                i += 1
            else:
                arr[k] = right_half[j]
                j += 1
            k += 1

        while i < len(left_half):
            arr[k] = left_half[i]
            i += 1
            k += 1

        while j < len(right_half):
```

```
            arr[k] = right_half[j]
            j += 1
            k += 1

# Example usage:
arr = [12, 11, 13, 5, 6, 7]
merge_sort(arr)
print("Merge Sorted array:", arr)
```

Quicksort:

```
def quicksort(arr):
    if len(arr) <= 1:
        return arr
    else:
        pivot = arr[0]
        less_than_pivot = [x for x in arr[1:] if x <= pivot]
        greater_than_pivot = [x for x in arr[1:] if x > pivot]
        return quicksort(less_than_pivot) + [pivot] + quicksort(greater_than_pivot)

# Example usage:
arr = [10, 7, 8, 9, 1, 5]
sorted_arr = quicksort(arr)
print("Quicksort Sorted array:", sorted_arr)
```

Binary Search:

```
def binary_search(arr, target):
    left, right = 0, len(arr) - 1
    while left <= right:
        mid = (left + right) // 2
        if arr[mid] == target:
            return mid
        elif arr[mid] < target:
```

```
            left = mid + 1
        else:
            right = mid - 1
    return -1

# Example usage:
arr = [2, 3, 4, 10, 40]
target = 10
index = binary_search(arr, target)
if index != -1:
    print("Element", target, "found at index", index)
else:
    print("Element", target, "not found.")
```

Backtracking: Systematically explores all possible solutions to a problem by incrementally building candidates and discarding those that fail to satisfy the problem's constraints. Applications include solving Sudoku puzzles, generating permutations, and solving the N-Queens problem.

Sudoku Solver:

```
def is_valid(board, row, col, num):
    # Check if the number is already in the row
    for i in range(9):
        if board[row][i] == num:
            return False

    # Check if the number is already in the column
    for i in range(9):
        if board[i][col] == num:
            return False

    # Check if the number is already in the 3x3 grid
    start_row, start_col = 3 * (row // 3), 3 * (col // 3)
    for i in range(3):
        for j in range(3):
```

```python
                if board[start_row + i][start_col + j] == num:
                    return False
    return True

def solve_sudoku(board):
    for row in range(9):
        for col in range(9):
            if board[row][col] == 0:
                for num in range(1, 10):
                    if is_valid(board, row, col, num):
                        board[row][col] = num
                        if solve_sudoku(board):
                            return True
                        board[row][col] = 0
                return False
    return True

# Example usage:
board = [
    [5, 3, 0, 0, 7, 0, 0, 0, 0],
    [6, 0, 0, 1, 9, 5, 0, 0, 0],
    [0, 9, 8, 0, 0, 0, 0, 6, 0],
    [8, 0, 0, 0, 6, 0, 0, 0, 3],
    [4, 0, 0, 8, 0, 3, 0, 0, 1],
    [7, 0, 0, 0, 2, 0, 0, 0, 6],
    [0, 6, 0, 0, 0, 0, 2, 8, 0],
    [0, 0, 0, 4, 1, 9, 0, 0, 5],
    [0, 0, 0, 0, 8, 0, 0, 7, 9]
]

if solve_sudoku(board):
    print("Sudoku solved successfully:")
    for row in board:
        print(row)
else:
    print("No solution exists.")
```

Generating Permutations: Generating permutations of a given list of elements is a common problem in computer science.

Here's a Python implementation of generating all permutations of a list using recursion:

```python
def generate_permutations(nums):
    result = []
    generate(nums, [], result)
    return result

def generate(nums, permutation, result):
    if not nums:
        result.append(permutation)
        return

    for i in range(len(nums)):
        # Choose the current element as the next element in permutation
        new_permutation = permutation + [nums[i]]

        # Exclude the current element and generate permutations of remaining elements
        generate(nums[:i] + nums[i+1:], new_permutation, result)

# Example usage:
nums = [1, 2, 3]
print("Permutations:", generate_permutations(nums))
```

Solving the N-Queens problem: The N-Queens problem is a classic problem in combinatorial optimization, where the task is to place N queens on an N×N chessboard such that no two queens threaten each other.

Here's a Python implementation using backtracking:

```
def solve_n_queens(n):
    def is_safe(board, row, col):
        # Check if there is a queen in the same column
        for i in range(row):
            if board[i][col] == 1:
                return False

        # Check if there is a queen in the upper left diagonal
        for i, j in zip(range(row, -1, -1), range(col, -1, -1)):
            if board[i][j] == 1:
                return False

        # Check if there is a queen in the upper right diagonal
        for i, j in zip(range(row, -1, -1), range(col, n)):
            if board[i][j] == 1:
                return False

        return True

    def solve(board, row):
        if row >= n:
            return True

        for col in range(n):
            if is_safe(board, row, col):
                board[row][col] = 1

                if solve(board, row + 1):
                    return True

                # Backtrack if placing a queen at (row, col) doesn't lead to a solution
                board[row][col] = 0
```

```python
        return False

    # Initialize an empty chessboard
    board = [[0] * n for _ in range(n)]

    if solve(board, 0):
        return board
    else:
        return None

def print_board(board):
    if board is None:
        print("No solution exists.")
    else:
        for row in board:
            print(" ".join("Q" if cell == 1 else "." for cell in row))

# Example usage:
n = 4
print("Solution for", n, "queens:")
print_board(solve_n_queens(n))
```

This implementation recursively places queens on the chessboard row by row, checking if each placement is safe. If a queen can be safely placed in a given position, the algorithm proceeds to the next row. If all queens are successfully placed, a solution is found. If no safe placement is found for the current row, the algorithm backtracks and tries a different column in the previous row.

Real-world examples of data structures and algorithms

- **Social Networks:** Graph data structures and algorithms are used extensively in social networks to model connections between users, suggest friends, and analyze network properties.

- **Web Search Engines:** Search algorithms (e.g., depth-first search, breadth-first search) and data structures (e.g., hash tables, inverted indexes) play a crucial role in indexing and retrieving web pages efficiently.

- **Computer Graphics:** Data structures such as trees and graphs are used to represent hierarchical structures (e.g., scene graphs), while algorithms like depth-first search and breadth-first search are used for traversal and rendering.

- **Databases:** Data structures like B-trees and hash tables are used for indexing and organizing data efficiently in databases. Sorting algorithms (e.g., merge sort, quicksort) are used for sorting large datasets.

- **Routing Algorithms:** Graph algorithms such as Dijkstra's algorithm and A* search algorithm are used in computer networks and GPS navigation systems for finding the shortest path between nodes.

Close this chapter knowing that every challenge overcome is an achievement, and every solution is a step toward mastery.

Your code is the melody that gives life to projects. May they continue creating and programming with passion!

Thank you for allowing me to be part of your journey.

With gratitude,
Hernando Abella
Author of Data Structures and Algorithms in Python

Discover Other Useful Resources at:
www.beat-byte-publishing.com/

Get your Bonus Books at:

www.hernandoabella.com

ALUNA PUBLISHING HOUSE

Thank you for trusting our Publishing House. If you could evaluate our work and give us a review on Amazon, we would appreciate it very much!
Scan this code to leave an honest review:

Or go to:
https://www.amazon.com/review/create-review/?ie=UTF8&channel=glance-detail&asin=B0CVTLX8GS
Thanks (again!)

This Book may not be copied or printed without the permission of the author.
COPYRIGHT 2024 ALUNA PUBLISHING HOUSE

Made in the USA
Columbia, SC
04 December 2024

6b553ad4-6056-455d-a2de-dc3b01bbed86R01